LUCY, LUCY!

Are you ready to meet

LUCY BRONZE?

The awesome England full-back is one of
the finest players in the women's game and
a multiple winner of the **Women's Super
League** and the **Champions League**.

FOOTBALL SUPERSTARS

BRONZE

RULES

Hi, pleased to meet you.

We hope you enjoy our book about Lucy Bronze!

WELBECK

SIMON   DAN

I'm **VARbot** with all the facts and stats!

THIS IS A WELBECK CHILDREN'S BOOK
Published in 2022 by Welbeck Children's Books Limited
An imprint of the Welbeck Publishing Group
20 Mortimer Street, London W1T 3JW
Text © 2022 Simon Mugford
Design & Illustration © 2022 Dan Green
ISBN: 978-1-78312-637-8

Writer: Simon Mugford
Designer and Illustrator: Dan Green
Design manager: Sam James
Commissioning editor: Suhel Ahmed
Production: Arlene Alexander

A catalogue record for this book is available from the British Library.

Printed in the UK
10 9 8 7 6 5 4 3 2 1

Statistics and records correct as of June 2022

FOOTBALL SUPERSTARS

BRONZE

RULES

SIMON MUGFORD   DAN GREEN

CONTENTS

CHAPTER 1 - **WE LOVE LUCY!**.. 5

CHAPTER 2 - **TOUGH BY NAME**..13

CHAPTER 3 - **FINDING FOOTBALL**..29

CHAPTER 4 - **TRACKING BACK**.. 37

CHAPTER 5 - **TYNESIDE TO STATESIDE**.................................... 47

CHAPTER 6 - **LIONESS JUNIOR**..55

CHAPTER 7 - **TOUGH TIMES**..61

CHAPTER 8 - **WSL STAR**... 71

CHAPTER 9 - **HALL OF FAME**.. 79

CHAPTER 10 - **ENGLAND CALLING**..89

CHAPTER 11 - **LUCY IN LYON**... 97

CHAPTER 12 - **LIONESS QUEEN**...105

CHAPTER 13 - **BRONZE IS BEST**...113

Strength
Lucy uses her physical presence against opponents.

Speed
Lucy drives forward from the back at pace.

Determination
She has used injury setbacks to come back stronger.

Crossing
She delivers superb balls to her team-mates.

Tackling
Lucy is one of the finest at taking the ball off the opposition.

STOPPING – AND SCORING!
Lucy is an awesome defender, but she scores some **FANTASTIC** goals, too!

BRONZE IN NUMBERS

*Lucy has some **FANTASTIC** numbers to her name . . .*

2 . . . Lucy's **ENGLAND** shirt number

3 . . . **ENGLISH LEAGUE CHAMPIONSHIPS**

3 . . . **FRENCH LEAGUE CHAMPIONSHIPS**

3 . . . **WOMEN'S CHAMPIONS LEAGUE** wins

4 ... **DOMESTIC CUP** wins

87 ... **CAPS** and **9 GOALS** for **ENGLAND**

1 ... **FIFA BEST** Women's Player Award

1 ... **UEFA** Women's Player of the Year Award

AN INSPIRATION TO **MILLIONS** OF YOUNG FOOTBALLERS!

BRONZE I.D

NAME: *Lucia Roberta **Tough** Bronze*

DATE OF BIRTH: *28 October 1991*

PLACE OF BIRTH: *Berwick-upon-Tweed, England*

HEIGHT: *1.72 m*

POSITION: *Defender/Full-back*

CLUBS: *Sunderland, Everton, Liverpool, Manchester City (2014-17), Olympique Lyonnais, Manchester City (2020-22)*

NATIONAL TEAM: *England*

LEFT OR RIGHT-FOOTED: *Right*

Lucy Bronze was was born in **1991** in Berwick-upon-Tweed, a town in northern **England.**

Edinburgh

SCOTLAND

Berwick-upon-Tweed

Sunderland

ENGLAND

Liverpool

Manchester

WALES

Birmingham

Norwich

Swansea

LONDON

Brighton

Plymouth

Berwick is England's most **northern town.**

It's very close to the border with **Scotland!**

For a time, Lucy and her family lived on the island of **Lindisfarne.**

Also known as
Holy Island

It's a wild and remote place, famous its legends and tales of **medieval monks, pilgrims** and battles with the **Vikings.**

The spectacular *Lindisfarne Gospels* were created by a monk called *Eadfrith* around 700 CE.

The people from this part of the world are **tough** - just like Lucy!

MEET THE BRONZES

There is her dad, **Joaquin . . .**

He's from Portugal!

And her mum, **Diane . . .**

She was a teacher

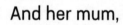

Diane's maiden name (her surname before she was married) is **Tough.** It's also Lucy's middle name!

18

Lucy has an older brother, **Jorge**

Her football rival

And a younger sister called **Sophie.**

Auntie Julie

(Lucy's mum's sister)

She helped Lucy to get into football!

Lucy was a **VERY** active little girl.

She could ride a bike
when she was **TWO** . . .

And whatever Lucy's brother Jorge did,

She wanted to do, too. But Lucy wanted

to do it **better!**

And that included . . .

FOOTBALL!

Lucy loved playing football more than any other game. And she was **really, REALLY** good . . .

She could **run** with the ball . . .

She could **score** goals . . .

GOAL!

But most of all, Lucy wasn't afraid to **tackle!**

Another thing Lucy is good at is **MATHS.**

She wanted to be an accountant when she grew up!

Lucy was quite **shy** when she was a little girl. She didn't like putting her hand up in class, or meeting new people.

24

But on the **football pitch,** none of that mattered. Lucy was part of a team. She felt **confident** and focused on playing the game she loved.

Lucy was **VERY** competitive. She was determined to **WIN** at everything.

Her **hair** got in the way when she played football . . . so she cut it short.

Lucy once played a **tennis tournament** in her football kit, because it was more comfortable.

"I'VE ALWAYS HAD IT . . . COMPETING WITH MY BROTHER AND SISTER FROM SUCH A YOUNG AGE . . . ALWAYS TRYING TO BE CONFIDENT IN MYSELF; I KNOW WHAT A DIFFERENCE THAT MAKES."

Lucy Bronze

CHAPTER 3

FINDING FOOTBALL

Lucy's brother Jorge played for their local club, **Alnwick Town.** So when she was **SIX,** Lucy joined, too.

Lucy's **mum** and her **Auntie Julie** took her to training and matches.

Lucy was the **ONLY** girl in the team! But before long she was much, **MUCH** better than any of the boys she played with.

She once tackled a boy so hard, it made him **cry!**

WAAAH!

When Lucy turned **12,** she was told that she **couldn't** play in a boys' team anymore.

So Auntie Julie and her mum found a place in the academy at **Sunderland** – 50 miles away.

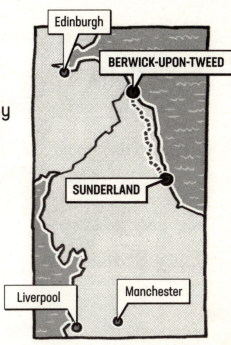

Lucy's dad took her to training after school **three** nights a week. They spent a **lot** of time in the car!

Lucy also played for **Blyth Town** as a teenager. She was a striker back then. There she met another Lucy – **Lucy Staniforth.**

They won lots of trophies at **Blyth** and have been friends ever since.

The two Lucys play alongside each other for **England**.

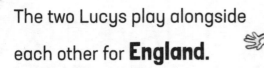

TO YOU LUCY!

THANKS BRONZY!

FOMP!

Staniforth plays for the club side *Manchester United!*

"ALL I'D HAVE TO DO WAS KICK THE BALL OVER TO HER AND SHE WOULD BULLY EVERYONE OUT THE WAY AND STICK IT IN THE GOAL."

Lucy Staniforth on playing with Lucy

CHAPTER 4

TRACKING BACK

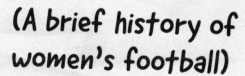

(A brief history of women's football)

Dick, Kerr Ladies was a team from Preston, England formed in **1917.** They played against both men's and women's teams.

In 1920, the team played St Helens Ladies in front of **53,000** fans at Everton's **Goodison Park.**

This record crowd for a women's game in England stood for **98 years.**

In **1921,** with women's football sometimes drawing bigger crowds than the men's game, the English Football Association **BANNED** women's football from its clubs.

So women's football formed its own association and carried on playing! In **1922,** The Dick, Kerr Ladies team even went on a successful tour of the **USA.**

In the **1970s,** things began to change.

The English FA *finally* lifted its ban.

A women's league in **Italy** featured part-time

professional players for the first time.

In 1971, France and the Netherlands played the first **OFFICIAL** women's international match.

France won 4-0

The first **OFFICIAL** international tournament - the AFC Women's Championship - was held in Hong Kong in **1975.**

The women's **EUROS** began in **1984.**

Sweden won, but Germany have won it

EIGHT times since.

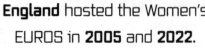

England hosted the Women's EUROS in **2005** and **2022.**

The first women's **World Cup** was held in China in 1991. It was won by the **USA.**

Mia Hamm

Lucy, with England, reached the *2019* World Cup semi-final — more on this later!

WOMEN'S LEAGUES TIMELINE

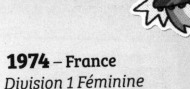

1968 – Italy
Serie A Femminile

1974 – France
Division 1 Féminine

1988 – Spain
Primera Iberdrola

1990 – Germany
Frauen-Bundesliga

BIRGIT PRINZ,
Frankfurt / Germany

2010 – England
Women's Super League

ALEX SCOTT,
Arsenal / England

2012 – USA
National Women's Soccer League

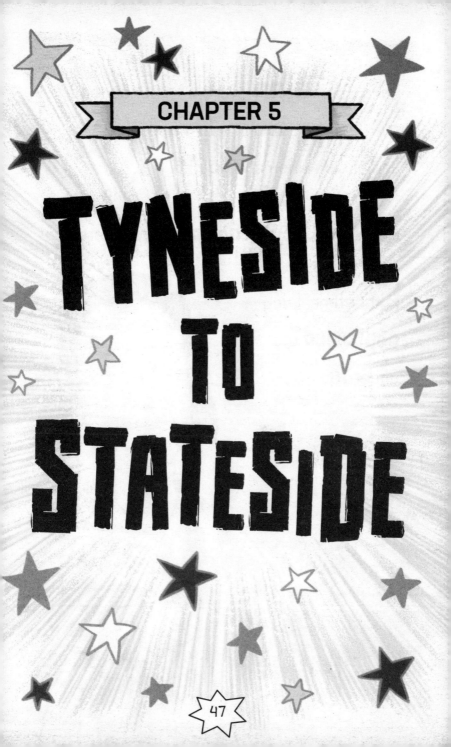

CHAPTER 5

TYNESIDE TO STATESIDE

Lucy Spent **EIGHT** years with Sunderland, starting in the **under-12s** and joining the senior side when she was **16.**

Her friend **Lucy Staniforth** was there, too!

In that time, Lucy **captained** the under-16s . . .

In her debut season with the first team she was **Manager's Player of the Year** 2007-08 . . .

and, aged 17, was named **Player of the Match** in the 2009 **FA Women's Cup final.**

Sunderland lost **2-1** to Arsenal.

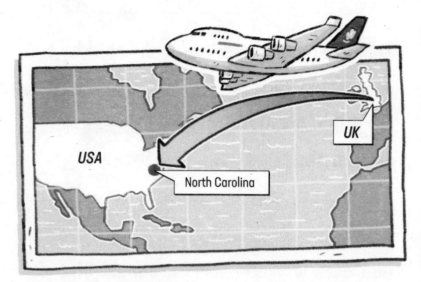

In the summer of 2009, Lucy was awarded a scholarship to the **University of North Carolina**.

The **USA** has been the top country for women's soccer* for many years, and Lucy was going to play for the **North Carolina Tar Heels,** one of the best college teams in North America.

BLAM!

*Football is called **soccer** in the USA!

Many top women's footballers have played for the **North Carolina Tar Heels,** including:

Legendary US striker

Mia Hamm . . .

US goalkeeper

Ashlyn Harris . . .

US winger
Crystal Dunn . . .

England coach
Sarina Wiegman.

With the Tar Heels, Lucy
became the first British player
to win the **NCAA Cup**, the US
college soccer championship.

"IF YOU WANT TO TURN INTO AN ELITE PLAYER, YOU HAVE TO EMBRACE COMPETITION. LUCY TICKS EVERY SINGLE BOX."

North Carolina Tar Heels coach Anson Dorrance
(A legend in US women's soccer)

CHAPTER 6

LIONESS JUNIOR

LUCY'S ENGLAND YOUTH HIGHLIGHTS

When Lucy was 15 and playing for **Blyth Town,** she got a call-up for the **England under-17s.**

IT WAS A FANTASTIC HONOUR!

FIFA WOMEN'S U-17 WORLD CUP

2008, NEW ZEALAND

FOURTH PLACE

UEFA WOMEN'S UNDER-19 CHAMPIONSHIP

2009, BELARUS

WINNERS

UEFA WOMEN'S UNDER-19 CHAMPIONSHIP

2010, MACEDONIA

RUNNERS-UP

FIFA WOMEN'S U-20 WORLD CUP

2010, GERMANY

GROUP STAGE

Lucy could have played for **Portugal** because that's where her dad is from.

OLÁ

The **Portuguese FA** asked her when she was **16!**

Around the age of **20,** Lucy missed out on call-ups to the **England senior side.**

So, she thought about playing for **Portugal . . .**

But **England** fans are very glad that she didn't!

LUCY, LUCY!

Lucy's Dad is an *England* fan, even though he's *Portuguese*.

"DAD SUPPORTS WHO HE'S TOLD TO!"

CHAPTER 7

TOUGH TIMES

In **2010,** when Lucy returned from the **USA,** she suffered a serious knee **injury.**

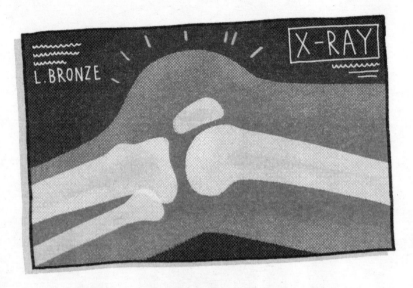

Lucy was on **crutches** for nearly a year and spent lots of time in hospital having **operations** on her knee.

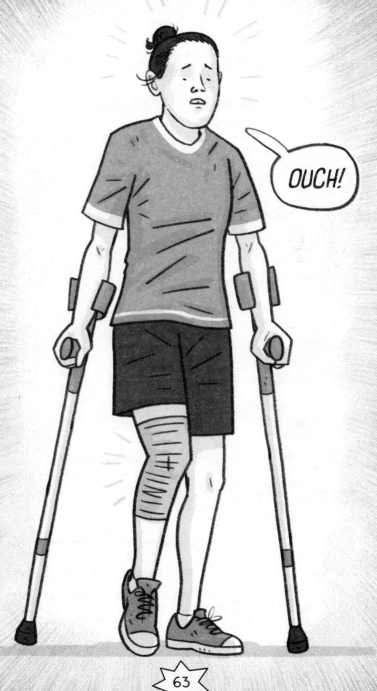

A professional **MALE** player would have team doctors, support – and lots of money to pay for it all.

It was very different in **WOMEN'S** football. Lucy had a part-time contract with **Everton,** but not much else . . .

SO, LUCY BECAME A STUDENT.

She went to university in *Leeds,* to study *sports science.*

At university, Lucy **worked hard** on her studies . . .

She made **new friends** . . .

She worked in a **pizza takeaway** . . .

WHOAH!

And in a café at a **five-a-side football centre . . .**

But all she really wanted to do . . . **was play**

FOOTBALL!

BOP!
BOP!
BOP!

Lucy needed to **kick-start** her career.

So, she created her own **training programme** to **recover** from her knee injury.

Her degree in *sports science* helped with this!

What do you say to a slow tomato?

KETCHUP!

Cheeky!

"NOTHING WAS AS PROFESSIONAL AS IT IS NOW, SO I JUST GOT LEFT TO MY OWN DEVICES. I DIDN'T REALLY KNOW WHAT I WAS DOING."

Lucy, on getting herself fit again

CHAPTER 8

WSL STAR

In **2011,** Lucy was back, playing for **Everton** in the **Women's Super League** - the **ALL-NEW TOP DIVISION** for women in England.

After two seasons, Lucy switched to Everton's **BIG rivals - LIVERPOOL!**

We said she was tough.

It was a good move –
Lucy won the **WSL**
with Liverpool in both
2013 and **2014**.

And she ended 2014 as the **PFA Women's Players' Player of the Year.**

For the **2015 season,** Lucy joined **MANCHESTER CITY.** The club were building a team to match the success of the men's' side.

It included Lucy's **England** team-mates . . .

. . . ace winger
Toni Duggan

. . . super centre-back
Steph Houghton

. . . magic midfielder
Jill Scott

With Lucy at the back, City's defence was **AWESOME.** In **2016,** they went unbeaten in the league as City won their first **WSL** title.

City only conceded **FOUR** league goals in their title-winning season.

Lucy also scored some important goals, including a headed winner in the **2016 WSL Cup final.**

BOFF!

And in both legs of City's first *Champions League* games against the Russian side Zvezda Perm.

LUCY IN THE WSL 2011-17

SEASON	TEAM	GAMES	GOALS
2011	EVERTON	6	0
2012	EVERTON	11	2
2013	LIVERPOOL	14	1
2014	LIVERPOOL	14	2
2015	MAN CITY	11	2
2016	MAN CITY	16	2
2017	MAN CITY	7	1

CHAPTER 9

HALL OF FAME

LEGENDS OF WOMEN'S FOOTBALL, PAST AND PRESENT

ADA HEGERBERG

COUNTRY: **NORWAY**

POSITION: **FORWARD**

YEARS: **2010-PRESENT**

All-time **Champions League** top scorer

Ballon-d'Or winner **2018**

The first ever women's **Ballon d'Or!**

MIA HAMM

COUNTRY: *USA*

POSITION: *FORWARD*

YEARS: *1989-2004*

Won **two** World Cups (1991, 1999)

Scored **158 goals** in **276 games** for the USA

MEGAN RAPINOE

COUNTRY: *USA*

POSITION: *MIDFIELDER*

YEARS: *2005-PRESENT*

Won **two** World Cups (2015, 2019)

Ballon d'Or winner **2019**

MARTA

COUNTRY: **BRAZIL**

POSITION: **FORWARD**

YEARS: **2000-PRESENT**

Top World Cup scorer, male or female (**17 goals**)

Six-times Best FIFA Player Award winner

SAM KERR

COUNTRY: **AUSTRALIA**

POSITION: **FORWARD**

YEARS: **2008-PRESENT**

Golden Boot winner in three different leagues

All-time **top scorer** in the USA's **NWSL**

LILY PARR

COUNTRY: *ENGLAND*

POSITION: *FORWARD*

YEARS: *1919-1951*

Women's football pioneer with **Dick, Kerr Ladies**

According to legend, scored more than **900 goals** in **30 years**

LINDA MEDALEN

COUNTRY: **NORWAY**

POSITION: **FORWARD/DEFENDER**

YEARS: **1981-2006**

Scored **64 goals** in **152 games** for Norway

Won **EURO 1993** and **1995 World Cup**

CARLI LLOYD

COUNTRY: *USA*

POSITION: *FORWARD*

YEARS: *1999-2021*

Won **two** World Cups (2015, 2019)

Scored a famous **hat-trick** in the **2015** World Cup final

BIRGIT PRINZ

COUNTRY: *GERMANY*

POSITION: *FORWARD*

YEARS: *1993-2011*

Won FIVE **EUROS** and two **World Cups**

Winner of **NINE** Bundesliga titles

All-time Netherlands top scorer (**92 goals**), male or female

VIVIANNE MIEDEMA

COUNTRY: *NETHERLANDS*

POSITION: *FORWARD*

Won **EURO 2017**

YEARS: *2011-PRESENT*

LIEKE MARTENS

COUNTRY: *NETHERLANDS*

POSITION: *MIDFIELDER / WINGER*

YEARS: *2009-PRESENT*

Won a **TREBLE** with Barcelona in 2021

Voted **FIFA Best Player 2017**

WENDIE RENARD

COUNTRY: *FRANCE*

POSITION: *DEFENDER*

YEARS: *2006-PRESENT*

Won **SEVEN** Champions League titles

Won **14** French League titles in a row

Renard has scored **33** goals for France – as a **defender**!

Helped PSG win a first **French league title**

CHRISTIANE ENDLER

COUNTRY: *CHILE*

POSITION: *GOALKEEPER*

YEARS: *2008-PRESENT*

Voted Best **FIFA Goalkeeper 2021**

ALEXIA PUTELLAS

COUNTRY: *SPAIN*

POSITION: *MIDFIELDER / WINGER*

YEARS: *2010-PRESENT*

Won a **TREBLE** with Barcelona in 2021

Voted **FIFA Best Player 2021**

CHAPTER 10

ENGLAND CALLING

26 JUNE 2013

INTERNATIONAL FRIENDLY

ENGLAND 1-1 JAPAN

Lucy's **England dream** finally came true when she made her **debut** for the senior team.

Japan were the **WORLD CHAMPIONS.**

At the time,
England's first
choice at right-back
was **Alex Scott.**

She's on the telly now!

So, Lucy had to **battle** for her place . . .

WORLD CUP WONDER GOAL

22 JUNE 2015

WORLD CUP ROUND OF 16

OTTAWA, CANADA

NORWAY 1-2 ENGLAND

This was Lucy's first ever **WORLD CUP.**

England had never won a **knockout match** in the competition.

Norway took the lead early in the **second half,** but **Steph Houghton** headed an equaliser.

BOMF!

Then . . . in the 76th minute, Lucy fired from just outside the penalty area . . .

It was a real netbuster — and it sent England into the *quarter-final!*

And Lucy wasn't finished! She scored the **winner** in the quarter-final, too, sending the host nation out of the tournament.

KA-POW!

It was the first England team, **men's or women's**, to be in a World Cup **semi-final** since **1990**.

England were beaten by Japan - the **defending champions** - but it was a **FANTASTIC** tournament for England.

LUCY HAD ANNOUNCED HERSELF TO THE **WORLD.**

"TO TAKE MY PLACE, SHE [LUCY] HAD TO BECOME STRONGER . . . FITTER . . . AND THAT'S WHAT SHE DID. SHE WENT AWAY AND BUILT HERSELF INTO A MACHINE, BASICALLY."

Alex Scott

CHAPTER 11

LUCY IN LYON

The French club **Olympique Lyonnais Féminin** (Lyon) are the most successful women's club in Europe, and probably the best side in the world.

Since 2007, they have won **15 French League titles** (a record) . . .

NINE French Cups

(also a record) . . .

And an astonishing **EIGHT**
Champions Leagues

(yes, that's a record, too!)

Including **FIVE** in a row

RECORD

And *THIS* was the club that Lucy joined in the summer of 2017.

Lyon described Lucy as the **BEST FULL-BACK IN THE WORLD** when they signed her, and she joined an awesome squad that included:

Sensational Norwegian striker **Ada Hegerberg . . .**

Captain of France
and Lyon legend
Wendie Renard . . .

And French goalkeeping superstar
Sarah Bouhaddi.

WHAT A TEAM IT WAS!

In her **first season** at Lyon (**2017–18**), Lucy won the **D1 Féminine** (French league) **AND** the **Champions League**.

Then, Lyon did it again the following season and added the **Coupe de France** to make it a **TREBLE**.

The club **repeated** the treble in **2019-20!**

LUCY'S **LYON** RECORD

2017-18

COMPETITION	GAMES	GOALS	CLEAN SHEETS
D1 FÉMININE	20	2	16
CHAMPIONS LEAGUE	8	2	7

2018-19

COMPETITION	GAMES	GOALS	CLEAN SHEETS
D1 FÉMININE	16	1	12
CHAMPIONS LEAGUE	9	1	4

2019-20

COMPETITION	GAMES	GOALS	CLEAN SHEETS
D1 FÉMININE	15	0	13
CHAMPIONS LEAGUE	6	0	4

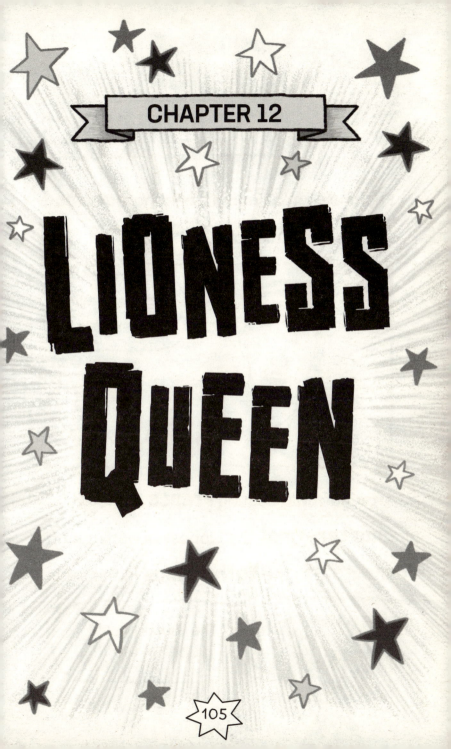

CHAPTER 12

LIONESS QUEEN

EURO 2017

THE NETHERLANDS

England won their group, beating **Scotland** (6-0 - oof!), **Spain** and **Portugal**.

After narrowly beating **France** in the **quarter-final**, the Lionesses went out after losing 3-0 to the **Netherlands** in the semis.

2019 SHEBELIEVES CUP

USA

England played in this mini tournament with the **USA, Brazil** and **Japan** - some of the very best teams . . .

AND WON!

WORLD CUP 2019

FRANCE

Another **BIG** tournament for Lucy and England. In a repeat of **2015,** Lucy scored another brilliant goal against Norway, this time in the **quarter-final.**

Appearing in their **THIRD** semi-final in three major tournaments, England faced the mighty **USA.**

But in a **VERY** tense match that included **Steph Houghton** having a penalty saved, England lost **2-1** to the reigning champions (and eventual winners).

There's always next time!

The current England team is the **strongest ever.** Lucy plays alongside some of the most talented players in the world . . .

ELLEN WHITE

POSITION: *FORWARD*

CLUB: *MANCHESTER CITY*

England's all-time top scorer

FRAN KIRBY

POSITION: *MIDFIELD/FORWARD*

CLUB: *CHELSEA*

Chelsea's all-time top scorer

LAUREN HEMP

POSITION: *FORWARD*

CLUB: *MANCHESTER CITY*

4 x winner PFA Young Women's Player of the Year

LEAH WILLIAMSON

POSITION: *MIDFIELD/CENTRE-BACK*

CLUB: *ARSENAL*

England captain

"I THINK MORE OF THE PLAYERS HAVE NOW GOT THAT HUNGER TO WIN THINGS AND A LOT OF US HAVE PLAYED A LOT OF TOURNAMENTS WHERE WE'VE DONE PRETTY WELL, GETTING TO SEMI-FINALS."

Lucy Bronze, speaking about EURO 2022

CHAPTER 13

BRONZE THE BEST

THE BEST

2020 was a very special year for Lucy. After

her huge success at Lyon, she was named

THE BEST FIFA WOMEN'S PLAYER.

"I'LL REMEMBER THIS MOMENT FOR THE REST OF MY LIFE."

She was the **FIRST** British footballer to win the award.

BOFF!

And the first **defender!**

LEWANDOWSKI RULES

LOOK OUT FOR

Robert Lewandowski won the men's award.

In the summer of **2020,** Lucy returned home to England, to the **WSL** and **Manchester City.**

In **2022,** Lucy was on the move again - joining **Barcelona** for a new adventure.

In her two spells at Man City, Lucy played **111 games** and scored **14 goals.**

"SHE IS AN UNRIVALLED TALENT AND HER ENDLESS INDIVIDUAL AND TEAM AWARDS ONLY SCRATCH THE SURFACE OF WHAT A SUPERB PLAYER SHE IS."

Manchester City coach Gareth Taylor

As one of the **very best women players** in the world, Lucy is an inspiration to millions young people - especially girls - as women's football keeps growing and growing.

BRONZE RULES!

HONOURS AND AWARDS

SOME OF THE TROPHIES IN LUCY'S CABINET!

NCAA WOMEN'S SOCCER CHAMPIONSHIP

2009

FA WOMEN'S PREMIER LEAGUE NORTHERN DIVISION

2008-09

FA WSL

2013

2014

2016

D1 FÉMININE

2017-18

2018-19

2019-20

COUPE DE FRANCE FÉMININE

2019

2020

TROPHÉE DE CHAMPIONNES
2019

WOMEN'S CHAMPIONS LEAGUE
2017-18
2018-19
2019-20

FA WSL CUP
2016
2021-22

WOMEN'S FA CUP
2016-17
2019-20

THE BEST FIFA WOMEN'S PLAYER
2020

UEFA WOMEN'S PLAYER OF THE YEAR AWARD
2018-19

QUIZ TIME!

How much do you know about LUCY BRONZE? Try this quiz to find out, then test your friends!

1. Where was Lucy born?

----

2. Which position does Lucy play?

----

3. Where is Lucy's dad from?

----

4. Which was Lucy's first senior team?

----

5. Which country did Lucy move to in 2009?

----

6. With which team did Lucy first win the WSL?

----

7. Name one team that Lucy scored against in the 2015 World Cup.

----

8. How many times did Lucy win the Champions League with Lyon?

----

9. Which England player is Lucy's friend from Sunderland?

----

10. Which year was Lucy voted Best FIFA Women's Player?

The answers are on the next page *but no peeking!*

ANSWERS

1. Berwick-Upon-Tweed, England

2. Defender / full-back

3. Portugal

4. Sunderland

5. USA

6. Liverpool

7. Norway, Canada

8. Three

9. Lucy Staniforth

10. 2020

LIEKE MARTENS:
WORDS YOU SHOULD KNOW

FA WSL (Women's Super League)
The top women's division in England.

D1 FÉMININE
The top women's division in France.

WOMEN'S FA CUP
The top women's knockout cup competition in England.

FA WSL CUP
The second women's knockout cup competition in England.

WOMEN'S CHAMPIONS LEAGUE
The top European cup competition in England.

Women's FA Cup

HAVE YOU READ ANY OF THESE OTHER BOOKS FROM THE
SUPERSTARS SERIES?

FOOTBALL SUPERSTARS

1 FOOTBALL SUPERSTARS
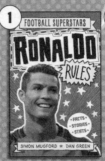
RONALDO RULES
· FACTS · STORIES · STATS ·
SIMON MUGFORD ★ DAN GREEN

2 FOOTBALL SUPERSTARS

MESSI RULES
· FACTS · STORIES · STATS ·
SIMON MUGFORD ★ DAN GREEN

3 FOOTBALL SUPERSTARS

KANE RULES
· FACTS · STORIES · STATS ·
SIMON MUGFORD ★ DAN GREEN

4 FOOTBALL SUPERSTARS

MBAPPÉ RULES
· FACTS · STORIES · STATS ·
SIMON MUGFORD ★ DAN GREEN

5 FOOTBALL SUPERSTARS

STERLING RULES
· FACTS · STORIES · STATS ·
SIMON MUGFORD ★ DAN GREEN

6 FOOTBALL SUPERSTARS

HAZARD RULES
· FACTS · STORIES · STATS ·
SIMON MUGFORD ★ DAN GREEN

7 FOOTBALL SUPERSTARS

RASHFORD RULES
· FACTS · STORIES · STATS ·
SIMON MUGFORD ★ DAN GREEN

8 FOOTBALL SUPERSTARS

VAN DIJK RULES
· FACTS · STORIES · STATS ·
SIMON MUGFORD ★ DAN GREEN

9 FOOTBALL SUPERSTARS

SALAH RULES
· FACTS · STORIES · STATS ·
SIMON MUGFORD ★ DAN GREEN

10 FOOTBALL SUPERSTARS

NEYMAR RULES
· FACTS · STORIES · STATS ·
SIMON MUGFORD ★ DAN GREEN

11 FOOTBALL SUPERSTARS

AGÜERO RULES
· FACTS · STORIES · STATS ·
SIMON MUGFORD ★ DAN GREEN

12 FOOTBALL SUPERSTARS

POGBA RULES
· FACTS · STORIES · STATS ·
SIMON MUGFORD ★ DAN GREEN

13 FOOTBALL SUPERSTARS

DE BRUYNE RULES

- FACTS
- STORIES
- STATS

SIMON MUGFORD ★ DAN GREEN

14 FOOTBALL SUPERSTARS

MANÉ RULES

- FACTS
- STORIES
- STATS

SIMON MUGFORD ★ DAN GREEN

15 FOOTBALL SUPERSTARS

SOUTHGATE RULES

- FACTS
- STORIES
- STATS

SIMON MUGFORD ★ DAN GREEN

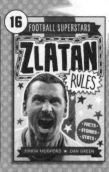

16 FOOTBALL SUPERSTARS

ZLATAN RULES

- FACTS
- STORIES
- STATS

SIMON MUGFORD ★ DAN GREEN

17 FOOTBALL SUPERSTARS

HAALAND RULES

- FACTS
- STORIES
- STATS

SIMON MUGFORD ★ DAN GREEN

18 FOOTBALL SUPERSTARS

MARTENS RULES

- FACTS
- STORIES
- STATS

SIMON MUGFORD ★ DAN GREEN

19 FOOTBALL SUPERSTARS

BRONZE RULES

- FACTS
- STORIES
- STATS

SIMON MUGFORD ★ DAN GREEN

COLLECT THEM ALL!

SPORTS SUPERSTARS

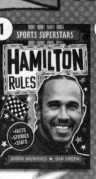

1 SPORTS SUPERSTARS

HAMILTON RULES

- FACTS
- STORIES
- STATS

SIMON MUGFORD ★ DAN GREEN

2 SPORTS SUPERSTARS

RADUCANU RULES

- FACTS
- STORIES
- STATS

SIMON MUGFORD ★ DAN GREEN

MORE COMING SOON!

ABOUT THE AUTHORS

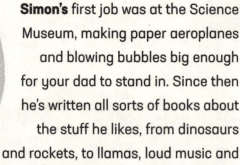

Simon's first job was at the Science Museum, making paper aeroplanes and blowing bubbles big enough for your dad to stand in. Since then he's written all sorts of books about the stuff he likes, from dinosaurs and rockets, to llamas, loud music and of course, football. Simon has supported Ipswich Town since they won the FA Cup in 1978 (it's true - look it up) and once sat next to Rio Ferdinand on a train. He lives in Kent with his wife and daughter, a dog, cat and two tortoises.

Dan has drawn silly pictures since he could hold a crayon. Then he grew up and started making books about stuff like trucks, space, people's jobs, *Doctor Who* and *Star Wars*. Dan remembers Ipswich Town winning the FA Cup but he didn't watch it because he was too busy making a Viking ship out of brown paper. As a result, he knows more about Vikings than football. Dan lives in Suffolk with his wife, son, daughter and a dog that takes him for very long walks.